History Insights

TUDORS

CONTENTS

Educational consultant: John Cook

Donna Bailey

Hodder Children's Books

a division of Hodder Headline plc

WHO WERE THE TUDORS?

From 1485 until 1603, all the kings and queens of England belonged to the Tudor family.

The Tudor reign began after the Tudors defeated the royal house of York and ended the Wars of the Roses. During the Tudor period, the king or queen decided how the country was run. They decided what form of religion the people of England should practise and who they should go to war against.

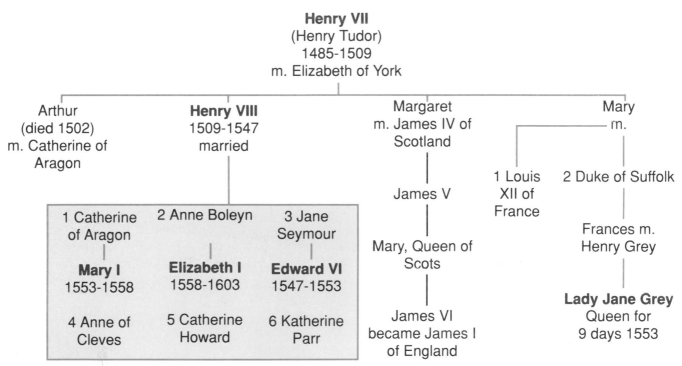

Henry VII
(Henry Tudor)
1485-1509
m. Elizabeth of York

Arthur
(died 1502)
m. Catherine of Aragon

Henry VIII
1509-1547
married

1 Catherine of Aragon	2 Anne Boleyn	3 Jane Seymour
Mary I 1553-1558	**Elizabeth I** 1558-1603	**Edward VI** 1547-1553
4 Anne of Cleves	5 Catherine Howard	6 Katherine Parr

Margaret
m. James IV of Scotland

James V

Mary, Queen of Scots

James VI became James I of England

Mary
m.

1 Louis XII of France

2 Duke of Suffolk

Frances m. Henry Grey

Lady Jane Grey
Queen for 9 days 1553

▶ Henry VII 1485-1509

Henry VII became the first Tudor king when in 1485 he defeated and killed the Yorkist king Richard III at the Battle of Bosworth in Leicestershire. Henry brought peace to the kingdom after years of fighting, known as the Wars of the Roses, between the House of York and the House of Lancaster. Henry was a Lancastrian, but brought the two houses together when he married Elizabeth of York.

▼ Henry VIII 1509-1547

Henry VIII became king of England and Wales at the age of 18. He enjoyed music and dancing and was good at sports. Henry wanted a son to take over the throne after his death, and he married six times. Only Jane Seymour, his third wife, gave birth to a boy who survived. During Henry's reign, the English Church broke away from the Roman Catholic Church and Henry became its leader.

▶ Edward VI 1547-1553

Edward VI was only nine when he became king. He was a sickly child and died after just six years on the throne. Edward was too young to rule by himself, so he was helped by his uncle, the Duke of Somerset, and later by the Duke of Northumberland. When, at the age of 14, Edward became very ill, he decided that his cousin, Lady Jane Grey, should be queen after him, instead of his Catholic half-sister Mary.

▲ Lady Jane Grey 10-19 July, 1553

Lady Jane Grey was Henry VII's granddaughter. When Edward died in 1553, 16 year-old Lady Jane Grey was made queen. She ruled for just nine days before she gave up the throne. She was later beheaded in the Tower of London.

▼ Elizabeth I 1558-1603

Elizabeth became queen at the age of 25. She was intelligent, charming and a skilful and popular monarch. She had a great love of clothes and jewels. Although various plans were made for her to marry, she never did. Elizabeth made the Protestant religion the official religion of the country. When her cousin, Mary Queen of Scots, plotted to kill her and seize the throne, Elizabeth reluctantly had Mary beheaded. Elizabeth's long rule brought peace and prosperity to England. She was the last of the Tudor monarchs.

▲ Mary I 1553-1558

Mary I's mother was Catherine of Aragon. After Henry VIII divorced her, Catherine was banished from court and Mary never saw her again. Mary was a devout Catholic and when she became queen, she was determined to make England a Catholic country again. She married a Catholic, Philip II of Spain, who was very unpopular in England. During Mary's short reign, over 300 people were burned to death because they refused to become Catholics, and Mary was given the nickname of 'Bloody Mary'.

CATHOLICS AND PROTESTANTS

During Tudor times, going to church was an important part of ordinary life.

The first English Bible was printed in 1535.

The church was normally the tallest building in a town or village and could be seen for miles around. Most people went to church on Sunday.

During the reign of Henry VII, all the churches in England and Europe were Catholic. However, people began to object to the way the Catholic Church was run. The Pope and the bishops were very wealthy and they made money by selling indulgences – pieces of paper people could buy which said that all their sins were forgiven. The people who protested against the Roman Catholic Church were known as Protestants. Throughout the 16th century, Europe became divided between Catholics and Protestants, and many wars were fought. These religious changes were known as the Reformation.

During this time, the monarch's faith was all important, and in England the Reformation took a special form, caused by a personal argument between Henry VIII and the Pope. Henry VIII and his first wife, Catherine of Aragon, had only one surviving child, a girl called Mary. Henry became anxious to have a son to take over his throne, and he fell in love with one of the ladies of the court.

As he was already married, Henry needed permission from the Pope to get a divorce. The Roman Catholic Church disagreed with divorce and this led to a quarrel between Henry and the Pope. Henry decided to break away from the Catholic Church and make himself head of the English Church. He divorced Catherine and married Anne Boleyn.

When Henry became king, England had over 600 monasteries, where monks or nuns lived and spent their time in prayer and study. Many monasteries were rich, and so when Henry became short of money, he decided to close the monasteries, sell off their lands and take their wealth for himself.

Archbishop Cranmer, who helped Henry get his divorce, was a Protestant who wanted people to read the Bible in their own language instead of in Latin.

He ordered that a copy of the Bible in English should be placed in every church.

◀ *Thomas Cranmer was appointed Archbishop of Canterbury in 1532*

▶ *Cranmer was one of the many Protestants burned at the stake during the reign of Mary.*

When Mary came to the throne, she brought back the Catholic faith and the power of the Pope. Many Protestants, including Archbishop Cranmer and hundreds of ordinary people, were burned during her reign. Her rule made many people fear and hate the Catholic Church, a feeling which lasted for a very long time.

When Elizabeth became queen, she made the English Church Protestant once more and named herself 'Governor' of the Church of England.

Protestants Protestants believe that Christians should read the Bible for themselves, and not rely on the priests' teachings. Protestant churches are quite plain, with bare walls and no pictures. The altar is a simple table, and Protestant ministers wear plain black gowns. They preach long sermons based on texts from the Bible.

▼ *Tintern Abbey in Gwent, one of the many monasteries that were destroyed by Henry VIII.*

Roman Catholics Based in the Vatican City in Rome, Italy, the Pope was, and still is, the head of the Catholic Church.

Roman Catholics believe that the Pope represents God on Earth. Bishops and priests help people understand and obey the teachings of the Church. Catholic churches are richly decorated with paintings and statues.

Fascinating Facts

During the Tudor period, people could face a fine for not attending church.

❝ Sire: The people of this town of London are murmuring about the cruel enforcement of the recent acts of Parliament on heresy which has now begun, as shown publicly when a certain Rogers was burnt yesterday. Some of the onlookers wept, others prayed God to give them strength, perseverance, and patience to bear the pain and not to recant, others gathered the ashes and bones and wrapped them up in paper to preserve them, yet others threatened the bishops. ❞

From a letter written by Simon Renard to Philip II, 1555.

LIFE AT COURT

Tudor kings and queens lived in grand style.

They built themselves great palaces and houses, and wore fine clothes and many jewels. The monarch and court would move from palace to palace at different times of the year.

The Elizabethan court could choose between several royal residences, including the Palaces of Whitehall, Richmond and Greenwich, Hampton Court, Nonsuch Palace in Surrey, and Windsor Castle. August and September was the time for royal progresses, when the monarch would travel around the country, staying in the houses of different noblemen.

Noblemen and gentlemen took part in tournaments on holy days, and on special occasions such as the king's birthday. Tournaments were fights or jousts between two knights on horseback carrying lances. Henry VIII enjoyed riding and jousted for 28 years until he was thrown from his horse and never jousted again.

▶ *Henry VIII jousting before Catherine of Aragon and her ladies at a tournament to celebrate the birth of Henry, Prince of Wales, who lived for only three months.*

▼ *Henry VIII put on so much weight that his suit of armour was enormous.*

> ❝ After dinner his Majesty and many others armed themselves . . . and he chose us to see him joust, running upwards of thirty courses, in one of which he capsized his opponent, horse and all. ❞

From a letter written by P. Pasqualigo in 1515.

◀ *The King's Lock was used to fasten the door of the king's bedchamber on royal progresses.*

Fascinating Facts

At least 500 people 'progressed' in Elizabeth's train across the countryside, in up to 30 coaches with 300 baggage carts and about 1000 horses.

Queen Elizabeth often used social occasions to discuss important matters with foreign visitors or her advisers. She was a skilful ruler and surrounded herself with faithful admirers. Her courtiers competed with each other for her attention. They gave her presents and wrote songs and poems in her honour.

The king or queen often went hunting the stag. In winter the court went hawking. Many noblemen had tennis courts and bowling alleys attached to their houses. Henry VII and Henry VIII both played tennis, but in Elizabeth's reign the game became less popular.

In the evenings after supper, the court enjoyed dancing, especially during the reign of Elizabeth, who loved to dance, even more than Henry VIII had done.

▼ *Elizabeth enjoyed dancing the volta, a dance in which the gentleman clasped the lady round the waist and lifted her into the air.*

▼ *Nonsuch Palace was built by Henry VIII.*

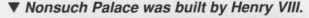

7

HOUSES AND HOMES

While the richest members of Tudor society lived in magnificent mansions, most people lived in one-roomed cottages.

Tudor mansions

Many of the richest Tudors lived in great country mansions, with a set of state apartments and a long gallery. These fine houses were built to show off their owner's wealth or to entertain the monarchs on their royal progresses. The gallery was the most important part of any large house. It was used for entertaining, dancing, games and as an exercise area when the weather was bad.

Big houses also had a large hall, originally used as a living and dining-room for all the family and the servants. As glass became cheaper, Tudor mansions were built with lots of windows that jutted out to let in light from three sides. Large houses had big formal gardens with paths and flower-beds bordered by low hedges. Taller hedges were clipped into animal shapes.

▲ *Many Tudor houses were of a black and white half-timbered construction, like Little Morton Hall in Cheshire.*

Manor houses

Manor houses were smaller than mansions. They were owned by rich farmers and small town merchants. A manor house had a hall downstairs where the family lived, a parlour which often contained the best bed, and a kitchen. Upstairs were three or four bedrooms, each leading off from the other. Other buildings, such as a dairy, bakehouse and brewhouse, were attached to the house.

Cottages

Most people lived in small houses or cottages in rural villages. They were often crowded with several families living together. There was a hole in the roof to allow the smoke from the fire to escape, and the floor was made of beaten earth. A loft under the roof was reached by a ladder.

▲ *Ornate mazes, like this one at Hever Castle in Kent, were a popular feature in the gardens of Tudor mansions.*

▼In Tudor times Bermondsey, now in the heart of London, was a small country village with thatched, half-timbered houses. This picture, painted in 1569, shows the wedding guests at a marriage feast.

9

FURNITURE AND FITTINGS

We know a lot about the fixtures and fittings in Tudor homes from pieces that have survived and from paintings of the time.

Tudor furniture was made mainly of oak, heavy, solid and richly carved. The hall of a manor house was furnished with tables, long benches, stools, iron candle stands, and open cupboards where silver was displayed. The household linen and clothes were kept in carved oak chests which also served as seats.

The walls of mansions and manor houses were lined with carved oak. Early Tudors had no pictures on the walls, but the wealthy hung up tapestries which showed scenes from the Bible.

Carpets were too few and precious to put on the floor. Instead they were draped over tables, beds and chests. The floor was strewn with loose rushes which gave out a sweet smell when trodden on. Some households had woven rush mats which could be taken up in one piece, cleaned, aired and put down again.

▲ *The Great Bed of Ware was for many years in the Saracen's Head Inn at Ware. It is over three metres long, three metres wide and nearly two metres high. It is richly carved on the headboard and the legs.*

▲ *The Queen receives two ambassadors from Holland in her Privy Chamber (her private office and sitting room). Three maids of honour watch, seated on cushions on the floor. The walls are hung with tapestries, and there is a woven rush mat on the floor. The Queen's chair of state is placed on a carpet and has soft cushions on the seat.*

◄ *Furniture was scarce in Tudor times. There were so few chairs that people sat on cushions on the floor, on stools or on benches.*

Wealthy people had large four-poster beds hung with curtains, which helped keep them warm when the fire had gone out. Bedrooms led from one into the other, so the curtains also gave the sleeper some privacy. Poorer families often had one large bed where everyone slept together. Most servants slept on straw mattresses on the floor with a log for a pillow.

Eating utensils were very simple. Poor people ate off wooden plates. Yeoman farmers and merchants had pewter plates. Every household had at least one knife, but not even the greatest palaces had forks. Guests often carried their own knives and spoons with them. There were no glasses so people drank from tankards made of wood, pewter, silver or gold.

Cottages had very little furniture. Poorer families usually had straw mattresses with coarse sheets, a chest, a couple of stools and a trestle table, an iron cooking pot, and a few wooden plates and tankards.

◄ *Tudor furniture was solid and heavily carved.*

▼ *The Great Hall at Cotehele House, Cornwall is furnished with a trestle table and benches. A large carved cupboard is at the far end of the hall.*

▼ *These pewter plates, a spoon and a tankard were used by sailors on board the Mary Rose.*

Fascinating Facts

When Elizabeth moved from palace to palace, her royal treasures, furniture and tapestries were taken with her.

FOOD FOR ALL

In Tudor England the wealthy ate well, but most people survived on a poor diet.

Foreign travellers often wrote about splendid banquets. These could have as many as ten courses and last up to seven hours. However, the guests only ate one or two mouthfuls of each dish, and the leftovers were finished off by the servants or given to the poor.

Most men and women lived on a much poorer diet. Cottagers and labourers ate mainly dairy products, bread and vegetables – peas, beans, turnips and cabbages – with the occasional bit of bacon, or a rabbit that was snared for the pot. In summer they picked wild fruits or ate fruit and vegetables from their small gardens.

Potatoes were not eaten in England until 1586 when Sir Walter Raleigh brought them back from America. Every large garden had a beehive as honey was the main way to sweeten food. Sugar was very expensive.

Ordinary people drank beer, but those who were a little better off drank ale. Wines from France were too expensive for most people. The only other drinks were milk and water.

Meat and fish were dried, smoked or preserved with salt for the winter months. Food was heavily spiced to disguise the taste and smell of decay.

▲ *Sir Henry Unton holds a banquet for his family and friends. The table is covered by a fine linen cloth, and each place is laid with a plate, a napkin, a knife and a spoon.*

❝ Every imaginable sort of meat known in the kingdom was served, and fish too, including prawn pasties and perhaps twenty different kinds of pastries, made in the shapes of castles, and of animals of various kinds, as beautiful as can be imagined.❞

A Venetian ambassador wrote this about a state banquet held in 1517.

◄*In humbler households, the table had no cloth. Only the father and mother sat on stools, while the children ate standing up.*

◄ **People cut up their meat with a knife and ate with their fingers. They washed their hands before and after a meal. This aquamanile or ewer was used to pour water over sticky fingers between courses.**

Fascinating Facts

About 1500 people attended Elizabeth's court. According to the Royal Household accounts, in one year they ate 60,000 pounds of butter, over 33,000 chickens, over 20,000 sheep and lambs, over 4,000 oxen, cows and calves, 310 pigs and 560 sides of bacon.

▼ **A banquet is being prepared in a busy kitchen. Joints of meat are roasting on the spit over the fire.**

FAMILY LIFE

Tudor families were usually large. Many children died at an early age and only one person in ten lived to 40.

Because of the high death rate, people often married more than once and a household might have the children of several marriages.

Generally, people married young. The average age for girls was between 14 and 16, and for boys between 18 and 21. Mothers and babies often died during or just after childbirth, but if the baby survived, it was wrapped up to protect it from cold and draughts. Because of the death risk, babies were always baptised as soon as possible.

As soon as they were out of baby clothes, children were dressed as miniature adults. Poor children did not have much of a childhood and were expected to work from a very young age. In wealthier families boys were often sent away to school at the age of seven.

Women worked hard in Tudor times. A good housewife not only knew how to look after her household and the servants, she made her own beer, baked her own bread, and tended the garden. She had to look after the bees, poultry and animals, make butter, cheese and candles, and preserves for the winter. She also had to know how to spin wool, to make and mend clothes and to embroider table cloths and tapestries.

> ❝. . .first sweep thy house, dress up thy dishboard, and set all good things in order within thy house: milk thy kye [cows], suckle thy calves, syc up [strain] thy milk, take up thy children and array [dress] them, and provide for thy husband's breakfast, dinner, supper and for thy children and servants, and take thy part with them. And to ordain [send] corn and malt to the mill, to bake and brew withal when need is . . ❞

From 'Boke of Husbandry' by Anthony Fitzherbert, 1523.

▲ *Women and girls were seen as inferior to men and many were treated badly by their husbands. If they disobeyed their husbands they might face the ducking-stool, a punishment for nagging or quarrelsome women.*

▶ *Lord Cobham, his wife, her sister Jane and his six children were painted in 1567. The children all wear their best clothes, like those of their parents. The children's pets include a monkey, a tame bird, a parrot and a small dog.*

◀ *These mothers are twin sisters. They are holding their babies, who are swaddled and wrapped up like parcels.*

Fascinating Facts

Bess of Hardwick rose from being the daughter of a small country gentleman to become the Countess of Shrewsbury. She was married four times and made a brilliant career as a merchant and farmer. Her household accounts tell us about her deals over cattle and pasture, about sales of wool, the feeding of her household, and the employment of her servants.

▶ *Bess of Hardwick.*

HEALTH AND HYGIENE

Tudor towns and villages were unhealthy places, piled with rubbish and riddled with disease.

▲ *Dung piles up in a village street, while a woman relieves herself in the stream. Another women empties a pail of rubbish out of an upstairs window.*

Tudor houses had no plumbing, so they were built as close as possible to a source of water, such as a stream or river. Raw sewage was allowed to pollute the water supplies, so even drinking water was a health risk. The outside lavatory was built over water or placed at some distance from the house. Indoors, people had chamber pots and stool rooms, where buckets were placed under stools with holes in the seats. The pots and buckets were emptied into a cesspit, a hole in the earth, but they created many unpleasant smells in a house.

Housewives usually emptied their rubbish straight into the street. People were supposed to clear the area in front of their houses. Workers called scavengers removed the dung in muck carts, but dunghills were still often left to pile up in the streets. Pigs, dogs and rats dug into the piles of muck, which became a breeding ground for disease.

The plague, a deadly disease passed on to people by rats' fleas, was an ever present threat. The worst outbreak in Tudor times was in 1563, when 17,046 people died in London. Another common disease was the 'sweating sickness', a kind of influenza, which came on very suddenly. Within 24 hours a patient could be dead. Smallpox and measles were serious new diseases in Tudor times. Medicine during the Tudor period was very primitive, and patients were often killed rather than cured by a doctor's treatment. Cures included dieting, blood-letting, and herbal remedies. Blood-letting, making a cut in a vein to let blood escape, was supposed to get rid of bad blood in the body.

▶ *Water carriers often sold water for use in cooking.*

Tudor surgeons carried out operations without pain-killers. They pulled teeth, set broken bones and amputated arms and legs while the patient was held down by the surgeon's assistants. The surgeon stopped a wound from bleeding by pressing a burning iron on it, or by pouring boiling oil over it.

This period was a time of change and experiment in medicine. Henry VIII founded the College of Physicians, and Elizabeth I gave permission in 1565 for the College to carry out human dissections. But only the rich could afford to pay doctors. Poor people relied on home-made herbal medicines to cure them.

> ❝To keep the teeth both white and sound, take a quart of honey, as much vinegar, and half so much white wine, boil them together and wash your teeth therewith now and then.❞

From William Vaughan's 'Delightes for Ladies', 1602.

◀ **Elizabethan women carried pomanders filled with herbs or spices to hide the unpleasant smells in the home or street.**

▲ **This surgeon's signboard shows that, among other things, the surgeon pulled teeth, cut legs and treated tumours and swellings.**

▲ **A doctor attends to a patient in his surgery. Notice the medicine bottles on the shelves.**

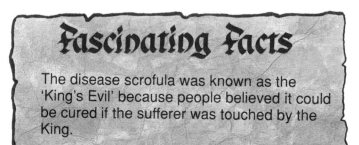

Fascinating Facts

The disease scrofula was known as the 'King's Evil' because people believed it could be cured if the sufferer was touched by the King.

COLOURFUL CLOTHES

We know a lot about Tudor fashions from paintings and writings made at the time. Some Tudor garments have even survived to this day.

Fashions in clothes are always changing. The Tudor age was no exception to this. Fashion trends were greatly influenced by the monarch and his or her courtiers. By Elizabeth's reign, garments were very elaborate. This was largely due to Elizabeth's love of fine clothes and to the new materials and precious stones that were brought back by explorers and traders now travelling to different parts of the world. Those who could afford them wore bright colourful silks, satins, velvets, jewels and feathers. However, while the wealthy wore splendid garments, the majority of the population wore coarse, ill-fitting clothes which were often full of dirt and vermin.

Men's wear

All men wore shirts. During Henry VIII's reign noblemen wore shirts with a narrow frilly band around the neck. By 1570 this had developed into the ruff, probably the most characteristic fashion of the period.

Tight-waisted doublets with a skirt were worn over a shirt.

With the invention of starch, ruffs got bigger and bigger, until by 1585 they were nearly 40 centimetres across.

Wide puffed sleeves were fitted close to the wrist.

After 1545 the short collarless Spanish cloak began to replace the knee-length gowns worn by noblemen.

By 1575 Venetian breeches, which were worn with separate stockings, were popular.

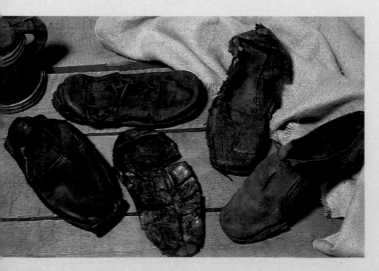

◄ These leather shoes were worn by sailors on board the Mary Rose. They are slashed to make them more comfortable to wear.

Women's wear

Under the influence of Elizabeth I, women's fashion underwent great changes. Women of all classes wore long dresses down to the ankles.

▼ Elizabeth was very proud of her long hands and wore beautiful gloves to show them off. These gloves, silk stockings and hat are thought to have belonged to her.

The hair was often frizzed, plucked back from the hairline and decorated with jewellery.

While early Tudor women wore caps covered by a headdress or hood, the later fashion for ruffs meant that Elizabethan women wore their hair up.

Waists were held in by corsets stiffened with wood or iron.

Low necklines were fashionable and were often concealed by a chemise decorated with a ruff.

The most typical women's garment was the gown and kirtle. The kirtle was worn beneath the gown which was often highly decorated.

The kirtle was made up of a bodice and a skirt. The pointed low-waisted bodice was characteristic of the later years of Elizabeth I's reign.

Wide skirts were held out by an undergarment made of wooden hoops called a farthingale. The Spanish farthingale was first worn in 1545. After 1580 it was replaced by the wheel farthingale.

Women wore shoes similar to men, often decorated with buckles or jewellery.

BEGGARS AND VAGABONDS

In the 16th century around half the population lived in poverty.

Beneath even the poorest labourers was a group of people who relied mainly on charity. They were known as vagabonds.

There were several reasons for people becoming vagabonds. Many had lost their homes and land when Henry VIII closed the monasteries. Some became beggars after losing their land when the large 'open fields' were divided up into small farms. Others became unemployed when the common land they had used to graze their animals was fenced in. Soldiers and sailors returning from the wars added to the number of homeless people.

▲ Elizabethans set up almshouses, like these in Ledbury, for the relief of the poor.

> ❝Where in all places throughout this realm of England vagabonds and beggars have of long time increased and daily do increase in great and excessive numbers . . . and daily insurgeth and springeth continual thefts, murders and other heinous offences . . .❞
>
> **From an Act of Parliament 1531.**

Gangs of beggars and vagabonds wandered from place to place, begging, stealing and terrifying whole villages. Many drifted to the towns, where they lived a life of crime. People became afraid to go out alone after dark, and carried swords and lanterns if they had to leave their homes. When a horde of beggars was reported to be on the outskirts of a town, people hurried into their homes, put up their shutters and barricaded the doors of their houses, barns and stables.

◀ Fools' masks were sometimes placed on the heads of wrong-doers while in the stocks.

Tudor kings and queens passed many laws to deal with the problem of the poor and homeless. Law-abiding people had to give alms, or money for charity, to pay for the old and those who could not earn a living because they were blind, sick or crippled.

People who were capable of work but lived as vagabonds were seen by many as sinners and were punished. Beggars without a licence were whipped. Vagabonds were branded and made slaves. All beggars, vagabonds and poor people had to stay in their parishes and not roam about the countryside.

▲ A vagabond is whipped through the street, to the enjoyment of the onlookers. Gallows in the background warn of a more serious punishment.

▼ Vagabonds were put in the stocks for three days and three nights and fed only on bread and water.

SCHOOLS AND SCHOLARS

Children's education in the Tudor age began early.

At home children were taught to say their prayers from a very early age. Most village children were taught the alphabet and simple arithmetic by the priest at the parish school.

At the age of seven, the sons of wealthy farmers and merchants often went to grammar school. There the pupils were taught English and Latin grammar, history, geography, arithmetic and to sing psalms. Children had to learn long passages of text by heart, and were often beaten or whipped. They worked long hours, from six until eleven o'clock in the morning and from one to six in the afternoon in the summer, and two hours less in the winter.

Many boys did not go to grammar schools, but became apprentices. An apprentice lived in his master's home for seven years with other apprentices, and learned a craft or trade.

A few boys went on to university at Oxford or Cambridge at the age of 15 where they remained for four to seven years.

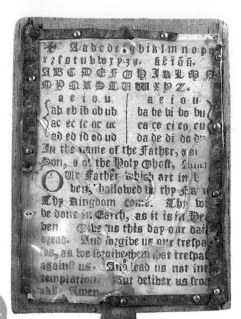

▲ A hornbook was a sheet of paper containing the alphabet mounted on a wooden board, and protected by a thin sheet of transparent horn. Horn books were also called criss-cross books because the first line started with a cross. Notice that the alphabet in those days did not have the letter j.

▼ Shakespeare was educated in this classroom at Edward VI grammar school at Stratford-on-Avon.

▲ Dame schools were schools in the teacher's home where children were taught the alphabet and reading.

❝The lady Elizabeth has accomplished her sixteenth year . . . French and Italian she speaks like English; Latin with fluency, propriety and judgement; she also spoke Greek with me, frequently, willingly and moderately. Nothing can be more elegant than her handwriting . . . In music she is very skilful . . .❞

From 'The Schoolmaster' (1570), by Roger Ascham, tutor to Princess Elizabeth.

Girls attended both the parish schools and the early years of the grammar schools, but women were not allowed to go to university. Most girls were expected to help in the home and become good housewives. The daughters of wealthier families often learned to read and write from parents, older brothers or governesses. They had visiting tutors for music, dancing and French. Children of the nobility, and of royalty were educated at home

▲ **This grammar school in Shrewsbury, Shropshire was built in the reign of Henry VIII.**

▼ **At least three classes appear to be in progress in this picture of a Tudor grammar school. One boy has obviously displeased one of the masters!**

MUSIC AND DRAMA

The Tudors loved making music and performing.

We know this through the paintings that have survived and the music and plays which are still performed today.

Henry VII's household accounts are full of payments to poets and musicians and payments for songs or for instruments. Henry VIII was an excellent musician. He had a fine voice, played several instruments and composed music as well. Edward VI played the lute, and both Mary and Elizabeth played the lute and the virginals (an early type of piano).

Men and women played instruments together, sang together, or played solo pieces.

▲ *During this musical evening, the flute and the lute are played.*

From right to left, the people in this painting are playing a viol, a recorder, a lute and a virginal. ▶

▶ *The lute was a popular solo instrument in the 16th century.*

Every rich family paid professional musicians to entertain their guests and to provide music for dancing. Guests were supposed to take part in the music-making after a meal, and felt ashamed if they could not join in.

At the beginning of the Tudor age, most plays were based on religious stories, and were known as morality plays. Strolling players wandered through the countryside, performing from the back of a cart, on stages built in the market square, or in the churchyard. In the reign of Henry VIII people enjoyed comedy plays, such as *Gammer Gurton's Needle*, a play about English village life. Tragedies were also popular, and often bloodthirsty. Women were not allowed to act in plays, so all the women's parts were played by boys.

The first two permanent theatres were built in London in 1576. By the end of Elizabeth's reign, large audiences watched the plays of dramatists like Shakespeare, Marlowe, and Ben Jonson.

Less well off people also enjoyed songs and ballads, and wandering fiddlers often provided music for a village wedding or a dance in a farmhouse kitchen.

◀ *Most Elizabethan playhouses were circular wooden buildings, like the Globe at Southwark, built in 1599. Shakespeare called it a 'wooden O'.*

▶ *By 1592 Shakespeare was earning money as an actor and playwright in London. He was so successful that he built one of the finest houses in Stratford.*

Fascinating Facts

Ballads were stories about popular events put to music. Many of our nursery rhymes go back to ballads popular in Tudor times. Characters like Mother Hubbard, Tom Thumb, Jack Spratt, Margery Daw and little Tommy Tucker were already well known.

SPORTS AND PASTIMES

Ordinary people worked hard in Tudor times and there was little time for sports and amusements.

The only time most people had for leisure was on Sundays, holy days, and festivals.

The twelve days of Christmas were a general time for feasting and relaxation. At these times mummers, people dressed up in disguise, paraded around the streets on hobby horses, and acted out plays.

Villagers enjoyed country and maypole dancing on the village green at these festivals. Local games included tumbling, wrestling, hurling, archery, throwing the hammer, and cudgel play. In cudgel play, the opponents each had a heavy cudgel or stick and each tried to hit the other on the head first.

Violent, blood-thirsty sports such as bear-baiting, bull-baiting and cock-fighting were popular. London had many cockpits, and people bet large sums of money on which cock would win a fight.

Bear-baiting usually took place on Thursdays, in bear gardens or in cockpits. The bear was fastened to a post with chains. Fierce dogs were set on the bear and tried to tear out its throat before the bear could kill the dogs with its paws. Some people objected to this cruelty because of their religious beliefs.

◄ Cock fighting was a favourite sport in Tudor England.

Sunday was the day for football, which was a very rough game. Almost all the references to football in Tudor books, letters and plays mention someone being injured.

Indoor games included chess, draughts and backgammon. Many people gambled on cards or dice.

Fascinating Facts

On Shrove Tuesday, schoolboys were allowed to bring their fighting cocks to school to do battle in the school cockpit.

▼ This portrait of the third Earl of Windsor and his family shows two of the boys playing chess, and the other two playing cards.

▶ Country or 'round' dances were very popular at every level of society.

▼ This backgammon board was used by sailors on the Mary Rose, which sank off Portsmouth in 1545 and was recovered in 1982.

▶ On May Day the villagers went into the woods to cut a maypole. They put up the maypole on the village green and decorated it with leaves and flowers, then they danced around it. May Day is still celebrated in different parts of the world today.

TUDOR TOWNS AND TRADE

Tudor towns were small compared with today.

Most people in the Tudor age lived in the country. Except for London, towns were small. The centres of towns were crowded with churches and markets, houses and warehouses, shops, schools and pleasure gardens. The tall houses were built very close together, and the streets between them were narrow, unpaved, dirty and smelly.

By the end of Elizabeth's reign, London was the largest city in Europe, but it still had orchards, gardens and pasture land. Pigs wandered through the streets, and cattle were sold at Smithfield market. The streets were crowded with people – porters, water carriers, ballad sellers, sweeps, pie sellers and pedlars. Many of them called out to let people know what they were selling. Town criers shouted out news. Nightwatchmen patrolled the streets after dark calling out the time.

Shops increased in number and many shopkeepers became rich and important. Originally, goods to be sold were made in the room behind the counter, but as time went on, goods were brought in from outside.

Different trades and occupations usually gathered together in one part of the city and streets were often named after them. Skinners Lane, Goldsmith's Row, Fish Street, and Bread Street are street names still found in many towns today.

Merchants had to belong to companies or guilds. Guilds laid down rules for trade and controlled the prices and the quality of the goods made by their apprentices.

As trade with other countries increased, new goods became available – ivory, spices, silk, gold, furs and timber. Ships carried English wool, tin and other goods to all parts of Europe.

There were no shops in the country villages. Country people visited large fairs once or twice a year. Pedlars travelled from village to village to sell small items such as laces, ribbons, mirrors, toys and clothes.

◀ *A pedlar's tray was filled with exciting goods for sale.*

▼ *A farmer's wife sets off to market to sell her live poultry.*

▲ Sheep and cattle are driven to market at East Cheap in London, 1598.

❛This city of London is so large and splendidly built, so populous and excellent in crafts and merchant citizens, and so prosperous, that it is not only the first in the whole realm of England, but is esteemed one of the most famous in all Christendom.❜

From a description by Thomas Platter of Basle, 1598.

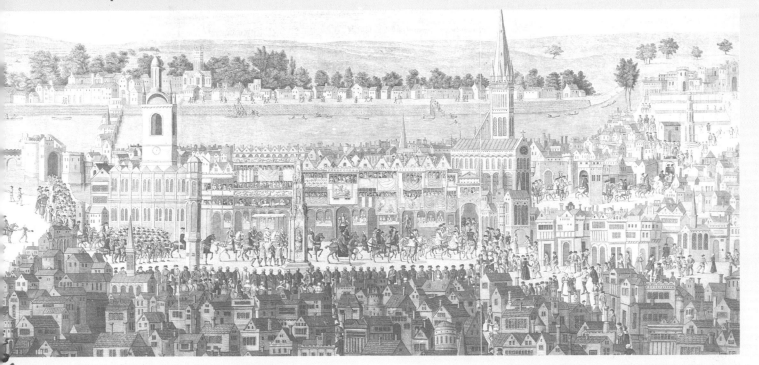

▲This picture of Edward VI's coronation procession from the Tower of London to Westminster shows that London was still a small town, with small wooden houses closely huddled together, and green fields not far away.

▶Ballad singers sold sheets of ballads in city streets, at fairs and at markets.

▲ A nightwatchman with his dog .

29

SHIPS AND SAILORS

The Tudor period was a time of exploration and discovery.

Columbus had sailed to America for the King of Spain in 1492, and adventurers were excited by the stories of the fabulous wealth found in the 'New World'. The first English expedition to America sailed in 1497. John Cabot landed on St John's Island, off the coast of Newfoundland, and claimed it on behalf of Henry VII.

Henry VIII built many large and powerful ships, and his ship the *Great Harry* was very famous. Her sister ship the *Mary Rose* sank as she was returning from a battle in 1545. Only 30 men of her crew of 500 were saved from drowning. Henry wanted to raise the ship to save her guns, but after three unsuccessful attempts, the idea was abandoned. The *Mary Rose* was not raised until 1982.

Skeletons, cutlery, musical instruments and bows and arrows were found when the ship was brought to the surface.

▶ *The ships of the Armada were thrown into confusion when the English sent fireships among the anchored fleet.*

◀ *Early explorers used a globe like this one.*

◀ *Sir Walter Raleigh, shown here with his son, organised many voyages of exploration to North America.*

▼ *A drawing of the Mary Rose made during the time of Henry VIII.*

Henry encouraged sailors to go on voyages. The main purpose of all these voyages was to buy and sell goods. English ships carried wool and cloth to Sicily, Tripoli, and Beirut. They brought back silks, wines, sweet oils, cotton, Turkish carpets, spices and wood. Other ships sailed to Africa, Russia and America. In 1577 Sir Francis Drake left Plymouth in the *Golden Hind* and became the first English sea captain to sail round the world.

Other countries, such as Spain, Portugal and Holland, were also trading with America and the Far East. The Spanish were very angry with Drake because he attacked their trading settlements and treasure ships on the Spanish Main (the northern coast of South America).

Drake's successes made him very popular in England. He was seen by many people as a Protestant hero fighting the Catholic king, Philip II of Spain. Spain and England by now were at war, and in 1588 Philip sent the Armada, a fleet of 130 ships, to invade England. The Armada was first delayed by storms and later attacked by the English ships as it sailed up the Channel.

Bad weather forced the Armada to anchor off the French coast at Calais. During the night the English floated some burning fireships in among the Spanish fleet, which had to scatter to avoid them. The next day a great sea battle was fought. A sudden gale allowed the remaining Spanish ships to escape into the North Sea. They sailed on round the north of Scotland and Ireland, where many ships were shipwrecked. Only 67 ships of the Armada returned to Spain.

It was a great victory for the English, and throughout Europe people believed that God had helped the English to win.

FASCINATING FACTS

Many new fruits and plants were brought back by English explorers, including tomatoes, potatoes and the Michaelmas daisy. Tobacco was brought from America by John Hawkins as early as 1586, and was made fashionable by Sir Walter Raleigh.

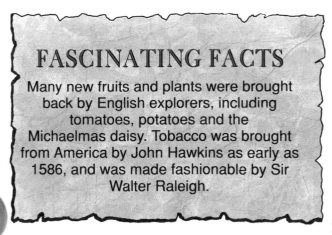

INDEX